"Too often in our chaotic and competitive world, leaders feel pressure to project a persona that hides how they are *really* feeling. In *Grace Notes*, John Baldoni shows leaders that being more of who they are is a superpower."

Tasha Eurich, Ph.D., *New York Times* best-selling author, *Insight* and *Bankable Leadership*

"In a crisis, the best leaders step up. In *Grace Notes,* leadership guru John Baldoni offers the practical advice he's learned from decades of coaching executives through tough times—presented in a poetic style and featuring his beautiful photographs. Read just one of these thoughtful entries each day, and you will soon be a more effective leader."

Adrian Gostick & Chester Elton, *New York Times* bestselling authors of *Leading with Gratitude* and *Anxiety at Work*

"*Grace Notes* gives me and us all hope and a feeling of calm, a reversal of the misfortune of conflict and sickness our world has endured. John has achieved what the poet Aeschylus once wrote that we all need more of. Through his book and wisdom, John has helped "[to] tame the savageness of man and make gentle the life of this world."

Louis Carter, CEO and founder of Best Practice Institute and Most Loved Workplaces, author of over 11 books on leadership and management, including *In Great Company* and *Change Champions*

"John Baldoni's *Grace Notes* with insights on leadership in the face of fear, isolation, and anxiety is a quick read to internalize and synthesize the essence of what truly matters in leading self and others during and after Covid."

David Nour, bestselling author of *Relationship Economics, Co-Create* and *Curve Benders* Thinkers50 Radar Class 2021

"John Baldoni's words of wisdom and compassion see in the challenges we face individually and as a society the hope inherent in reconnecting to what matters most."

Shannon Huffman Polson, author of *The Grit Factor: Courage, Resilience and Leadership in the Most Male Dominated Organization in the World*

"A wonderful series of simple reminders, refreshers, and inspirational thoughts from one of the world's most renowned leadership experts. With all of us challenged for time, John's insights take but a few moments to read but are timeless in their application."

Shane Green, CEO of LXbyDesign and author of *Culture Hacker*

"John Baldoni's *Grace Notes* is an invitation for leaders everywhere to explore the most challenging time we have experienced in the last hundred years -- navigating a world indelibly marked by a global pandemic. The book takes us on a sacred journey, exploring the highs and lows of transition, chaos and crisis. Through this poetic pilgrimage, we emerge better, stronger, and more enlightened about the possibilities we can create together. *Grace Notes* beckons our commitment to show up authentically and do our part to help ourselves, our organizations and our communities thrive in uncertain times."

Alaina Love, consultant, creator of the Passion Profiler,
and co-author of *The Purpose Linked Organization*

"John Baldoni explores the issues that overwhelm and concern leaders, particularly in times of crisis. *Grace Notes* is a collection of personal insights that -- taken together -- provide us all with welcome advice on how to act for the benefit of others, especially in turbulent times. There is no better time for us to pause and reflect on the grace that comes when we overcome anxiety and fear for ourselves, those we lead, and those we love…and help rediscover purpose and joy."

Jennifer McCollum, CEO, Linkage, Inc.

"John Baldoni manages to insert grace, symmetry, and poetry in a world of chaos. His work gives us license to stop and think while resting our brains and hearts. A must-read."

CB Bowman-Ottomanelli, MBA, MCEC, BCC, CMC
CEO, Association of Corporate Executive Coaches
CEO, Workplace Equity & Equality

Also by John Baldoni

GRACE: A Leader's Guide to a Better Us (2019)

MOXIE: The Secret to Bold and Gutsy Leadership (2015)

The Leader's Guide to Speaking with Presence:
How to Project Confidence, Conviction and Authority (2013)

The Leader's Pocket Guide: Indispensable Tools, Tips and Techniques
for Any Situation (2012)

Lead with Purpose: Giving Your Organization a Reason
to Believe in Itself (2011)

AMA Handbook of Leadership (2010)
edited by Marshall Goldsmith, John Baldoni and Sarah McArthur

12 Steps to Power Presence: How to Exert Your Authority to Lead (2010)

Lead Your Boss: The Subtle Art of Managing Up (2009)

Lead by Example: 50 Ways Great Leaders Inspire Results (2008)

How Great Leaders Get Great Results (2006)

Great Motivation Secrets of Great Leaders (2005)

Great Communication Secrets of Great Leaders (2003)

180 Ways to Walk the Motivation Talk (2002)
co-author with Eric Harvey

Baldoni Consulting LLC
Photography: John Baldoni

Quantity Sales Ordering: Order for US trade bookstores, wholesalers, and
organizations by contacting orders@lc21.com. *Special discounts are available
on quantity purchases by corporations, associations, and others.*

Printed in the United States of America
Library of Congress Control Number: 2021906265
ISBN: 978-1-7369467-0-1 (paperback)
ISBN: 978-1-7369467-1-8 (ebook)
First Edition

Mike

grace
notes

Leading in an Upside-Down World

Wisdom!

[signature]
7/21

JOHN BALDONI

To my grandson Tripp
to whose future this book is dedicated

CONTENTS

PROLOGUE

Because of Covid.
It's a phrase we heard a lot and with good reason.
Because of Covid we coped with a health crisis that has
disrupted our workforce.
Caused millions to lose their jobs.
And many jobs did not come back in their current form.
Our life was turned upside down.
Because of Covid is also a signal that we have learned.
We endured this crisis.
Despite not knowing when it would end.
But because of Covid we learned new lessons about ourselves.

We have strengths. We have resilience.
We have opportunities.
We have one another.
In many ways, we've pared our lives down to what's essential.
Our loved ones, our families, our friends, our colleagues.
Because of Covid.
While there is much to mourn, and much to fear, in our current world.
There are also new learnings, new opportunities... because of Covid.

It is said that when the British Army marched off the battlefield of Yorktown, a band played a drinking song called "The World Turned Upside Down."

True or not, the sentiment of the song rang true.

On both land and sea, the mightiest military had been defeated after an eight-year struggle with an upstart confederation of colonies (albeit with France's support) fielding an army that lacked the training, discipline, and weaponry of the more superior British force.

The fact that Britain could surrender a colony such as America was truly earth-shattering.

This story resonates with me looking back at 2020. The year turned upside down with the rapid spread of Covid-19, a pernicious virus that could infect and leave unaffected, or infect and kill. Resulting from the shutdown was an economic slowdown that threw millions out of work and hobbled our economy.

If that were not enough, the succession of killings of unarmed Blacks by white police officers became the catalyst for a massive movement for social change after the strangulation of George Floyd. Protests arced the nation and the world. Political discord fueled by conspiracy theories further added to our national divide. Adding to the misery were more hurricanes in the Southeast and forest firestorms in California.

Throughout the year, I created a series of short videos about the challenges facing leaders. The videos explored the emotions leaders were feeling and made suggestions for better serving their teams, their organizations, and themselves.

These thoughts are now collected in this book, *Grace Notes: Leading in an Upside-Down World*. The themes covered are fear, isolation, and anxiety and how we can overcome them with greater purpose and more joy.

The idea of *Grace Notes* dovetails with my interest in music.
A grace note can be ornamentation or flourish. It may also serve as
an "excuse" for misplaying a note—something I am very prone to do.
In jazz, grace notes are what give the harmonies their unique sound,
one that is spirited and unexpected. And in times of crisis, leaders
become like jazz musicians, improvising as they proceed and making
it look easy… as well as graceful.

While no one will want to relive 2020, what we learned in that
terrible year will make us better—more resolute, more resilient,
more compassionate. It was also a year of "grace notes," women
and men from every walk of life reaching out and helping others.

This book unfolds differently than my other works. My intention is to
let each piece speak for itself, that is, reflect the emotion of the moment.
Within the flow of the book there is an arc from darkness to light but
the progress, like life itself, is not linear. Ups and downs, high and lows,
all trend toward the light, though not in a straight line, toward a new
understanding of ourselves and our world.

While the messages contained here occurred in a terrible year, the
lessons they taught us are lasting and applicable for years to come.
I hope you find this collection of value in your leadership journey
as you create your own "new normal" for now and for your future.

I.

GRACE UNDER PRESSURE

Grace under pressure.
When I hear that phrase, what comes to mind is the five-alarm fire.
There's a lot of heat. There's a lot of noise.
And a lot of people scrambling around.
But if you look closely among fire and rescue trucks,
you'll notice a fire battalion chief,
with a very composed and collected demeanor, calmly giving directions.
Grace Under Pressure.

Grace under Pressure requires meeting
Anger with composure.
Denigration with respect.
Sadness with compassion.
Scarcity with abundance.
Insults with smiles.
Selfishness with selflessness.
Hoarding with generosity.
Life with gratitude.

Today everyone is looking for a leader who can exhibit
Grace Under Pressure.
Be collected. Be calm. Be composed.
This is someone that others can look up to be trusted.
Grace Under Pressure.

When the heat is on, good leaders step forward.
They demonstrate that they have what it takes to deal with the pressure.
They bring others along with them.
Grace Under Pressure.

DEALING WITH FEAR

We all feel fear from time to time.
And with good reason, mostly.
And so that presents a particular challenge
for those in positions of authority.
How do they navigate the landscape of fear?

The bottom line is they don't show fear.
They may feel it, but you don't show it.
You radiate calmness. You radiate confidence.
It doesn't come from arrogance.
It comes from a sense of caring for another person.
I want to be the go-to person for my people.
I want them to trust me.
That begins with radiating a sense of calmness about this situation,
that things will work out if we work together.

DISPLACEMENT

You are displaced from your place of work.
And for the first day or so, maybe that feels like,
"Hey, I can work from home."
But over time, you realize that you're working in isolation,
and that can be an unsettling proposition.

It is essential to have confidence in yourself.
If you were doing an excellent job in the office,
and you're following the task that your boss assigned you,
likely you're moving in the right direction.
Take heart. Stay close to your colleagues.
Seek feedback from your boss.
Do the best you can in the time that you have to do it.

HAVE CONFIDENCE IN YOURSELF

Confidence! Where does it come from?
It comes from your accomplishments, your achievements.
When you encounter something new,
confidence gives you that ability to muscle through.
But let's be honest.
Now we're in the middle of a pandemic and an economic crisis.
Who's been through that before?
No one that I know of.
But at the same time,
leaders who might be feeling a little less confident
—and that's not necessarily a bad thing—
need to take heart.

Trust your ability to pull your people through this crisis.
Trust what you can do.
And delegate authority and responsibility to those around you…
whom you know can excel.
This is an overwhelming crisis.
You will be judged by the decisions you make now…
and the actions you take as you follow through.
Trust your instincts.
Rely on your good people.
And you will succeed.
That will give you confidence as you go forward.

COPING WITH STRESS

I think all of us are feeling stress.
And that recognition is essential to coping with stress,
knowing that you're in the same boat with everyone else.
There are ways to reduce stress by focusing on your breath.
Breathe from your diaphragm, in and out regularly.
Breathe in through your nose.
Exhale through your mouth.
That will lessen the stress you're feeling.

Talk about stress, too
Get with trusted colleagues and talk about how you're feeling.
Share your thoughts.
Ideally, you'll come up with solutions that work for you, and maybe for others too.
It is helpful to recognize that stress is a natural reaction to uncertainty.
Acknowledge it.
Resolve to yourself that you will get better.
And if you feel you need to talk to a professional about it,
please reach out.
There's no stigma to feeling stress or anxiety, certainly not now.
There are lots of good people willing to help you.
All you have to do is ask.

BELIEVE IN YOU

In the tough times, it's pretty easy to become discouraged.
And that's human.
It shows that you have accepted reality.
And it's okay to cry.

Go outside and yell at the wind if you have to…
but eventually, you need to cope with what's going on.
There's a beautiful Japanese saying that says,
"Fall down seven times. Get up eight."

What that thought gets to is a concept called resilience.
All great leaders have been tested by their times.
The good ones—the ones we remember—overcame the adversity…
both personal and organizational.
They came out positively on the other side.
We, too, can do that.
Have faith in yourself.

TAKE TIME TO DELIBERATE

A colleague who was talking about how she wasn't quite ready to jump into the fray,
and determine what to do differently in the wake of this pandemic crisis.
As we were talking, I realized that,
while some people are already jumping in with both feet,
and thinking of new business models and new ways to connect with others,
some of us just need time.
You need time to process, and that's not a negative.
However, you react to the crisis, thinking and reflecting is positive.
Don't beat yourself up,
if you don't have a great solution to whatever is going on immediately.
Take your time.
Answers will come to you.

GRIEF

There is a topic we get too comfortable avoiding.
Loss!
Some people have lost a loved one.
And the grief they feel is real.
It's hurtful. It's painful. And that's normal.
For the rest of us, we have lost our way of work…
as well as our way of socializing with our friends.
That's a loss too. And it is okay to feel sad about it.
We owe it to ourselves to acknowledge this loss
and to process it in ways that are best for us.
If you're feeling isolated,
and feel you don't have anyone to talk to
reach out to mental health experts in your area.
Many are willing to listen.
Some of us can get by talking to friends… just talking out the issues.
It is good to connect with others.
Yes, we have loss.
But know that other people are there for you.

NEED FOR HUMILITY

I was listening to some commentary,
and a woman said that ours was a time for humility.
How right she is.
As we face this crisis, we know that it's greater than us.
A sense of humility allows us to look inward,
to see our own strengths as well as our weaknesses.
But also uncover ways forward.
Leaders must do what they can to assure their people
that they're doing what they can to make things better.
Everything won't be alright.
We are likely to be changed forever.
But in a way, it's a reminder of our humanity,
to be humble in the time of crisis.

TAKE CARE OF YOURSELF

In times of crisis, people get tired, very tired.
Leaders, too, get tired.
You want to do the best for your teams.
You are outward directed, which is good.
But don't forget yourself.
Your role is to be the best you can, of course.
But you can't be your best if you are too physically tired,
or mentally tired, to take care of your team.
Make some time for yourself.
Some of you may enjoy meditation and mindfulness.
Those kinds of things rejuvenate the spirit.
But also take time for family, of course.
Take time for friends.
Exercise, eat right… all of these things.
Self-care is essential for a leader.
Don't neglect yourself.
Because if you neglect yourself, you can't be at your best for others.

ANXIETY IN TROUBLED TIMES

Anxiety.

There's a lot of it and with good reason.

We are living in an upside-down world.

There is very little clarity about what's going to happen next.

We are in the grips of what is probably the biggest crisis that any of us have faced in our lives.

It is intimidating. It is natural to feel fearful and anxious.

Leaders must know when people are feeling anxious.

Give them permission to express it.

And to even own it.

Sometimes anxiety can be clinical.

And those instances you need professional help…

and there should be no shame in that.

Other times anxiety is just the feeling of unease that we feel.

It's important to acknowledge the subject.

Talk about it.

Provide help to those who need it.

But most importantly, realize that anxiety is a human reaction to uncertainty.

And as such, it's part of where we are in our world.

BE THE OPTIMIST

Half empty or half full?

If you're in leadership, you have to opt for half-full.

Leaders must look on the bright side of life.

You can say, Well, wait a minute.

We're in a world right now, which is coming apart.

The economy is in shambles.

We're fighting a deadly virus.

And we're torn apart by racial injustice.

What is there to be optimistic about?

That's a good question, and that's where it falls to leadership.
You have to be that person that rallies your people together.
Leaders who deal in optimism are not Pollyannas.
No, they are realists.
They look at the good side of life.
They realize, and they believe,
that there's probably more good than there is evil.
And they celebrate the right things, the kindness around us,
the good news stories.
But they also look inside the organization
to find out who's doing good things.
Who's achieving the metrics?
Who's helping others?
What teams are succeeding?
Find the optimism,
and you will find a reason to persevere.

NEXT FOR ME

Do I want to devote the rest of my life to what I'm doing now?
Or do I want to do something different?
These feelings are natural... and actually not unexpected.
But also they could be opportunities to re-think where you are now.
If you've had a successful career,
but you're looking for a new opportunity.

Or, if you've been stalled in your career where you are now,
and want to consider something different,
then this is an opportunity to reconsider.
There may not be that many jobs out there in the immediate future.
But when the situation changes,
consider new opportunities for yourself.
It may involve going back to school.
It may be looking for a new employer.
There are all kinds of things to consider.
So take heart.

LET'S BUILD TRUST

How does a leader earn trust?
Be transparent.
Share the information that you have.
Communicate clearly and consistently.
And part of that communication means you listen
and act on what you learn.
And part of that acting means you are decisive.
When a decision needs to be made, make it.

Finally, leaders need to hold themselves accountable.
And doing this, they set the example for others to follow.
In general, what trust does is promote a more caring
and more concerned culture.
And boy, do we need that right now!
Leaders need to pick up the slack where they can…
and make people feel that they're part of the organization.
Contributing, collaborating and belonging.

WHERE DO WE GO FROM HERE?

If you're in leadership, reach out to people in your company,
and find out what they would like to do differently.
What could we stop doing?
What could we do differently?
What could we do to make our company, our organization, more
strong and more resilient?

The future will be daunting.
But with the collective knowledge
and cooperation and collaboration of everyone on the team,
and everyone in the organization, we will succeed.
It is a leader's job to find out what people are thinking.
Challenge them to think.
We will make it.

RECHARGE & RENEW

Coaching, I like to say, is "Me Time."
Coming to an understanding of yourself by focusing on yourself.
Now more than ever we all need some "Me Time."
With this "Me Time." we can do one or two different things.

The first is to recharge ourselves.
We do this by connecting with people.
We can do it virtually.
Or we can do it with our loved ones with whom we're sheltered.
We also can recharge ourselves with exercise and recreation.

But there's another, perhaps more significant, opportunity—renewal.
Finding a new outlook on how you view life.
With the great challenges we're facing,
we are redefining the way we go to work.
We're also redefining the way we connect with other people.
Indeed, this is a time to begin again.
Recharge and renew.

SACRIFICE

Sacrifice is a word we don't often hear in times of abundance.
Now, in a time of scarcity, as we are all hunkered down,
sacrifice becomes a big issue that we talk about.
The challenge for all of us is to make our sacrifice worth it.
Whatever we're giving up — at minimum, we've given up our mobility.
We're staying in our domicile, so we don't pass the virus on to others.
Our challenge is to make our sacrifice, whatever it is, worth it.
So that we create a better tomorrow, something worth our sacrifice.

ISOLATION

There is a lot of loneliness going around.

Because people are not getting around.

How does a leader stay connected?

Virtual communications, sure.

But how about picking up the phone to have a conversation, not about work?

"Hey, how are you doing?"

"How are things for you?"

"Anything I can do for you?"

Reaching out like that proves that you're a boss who cares about that person as an individual and as a contributor.

II.

GRACE IN THE SUPERMARKET

Grace is a catalyst for the greater good.
It enables us to do better for our community, and our friends,
and ultimately ourselves.
Let me share a little story about a trip to the grocery store.

People were stocking up on supplies and the store was crowded.
I made it to the checkout lane only to realize I forgotten an item.
Going to get it meant walking all the way to the back of the store.
The young man behind me in line, sensing my hesitation, said,
"If you're late, I'll put your groceries on the belt for you."
"Really?" I asked.
"Sure, go ahead!"

As it turned out, I made it with time to spare.
And thanked the young man,
Later reflecting on his moment of Grace.

MAKE THIS YOUR FINEST HOUR

When Winston Churchill became prime minister in May 1940,
it was a surprise to a lot of people.
He was not well-liked.
Both parties viewed him as an opportunist,
but he wrote in his diary
that all that had come before had prepared him for this moment.
Ultimately it would be his "Finest Hour,"
as he navigated the Second World War,
notably in 1940 when Britain stood by herself
against hatred and Nazism.

Right now, you are pressed with challenges well beyond your control.
How you act now will determine if this will be your "Finest Hour."
Have faith in yourself that what you're doing now is the right thing.
Trust your instincts.
Trust your people.
Go forward.
Mistakes will be made, certainly,
but you will come out of it stronger and wiser.

CHANNEL YOUR ANGER

Anger!
There's a lot of it and with good reason.
The pandemic seems to stretch on.
We all feel economic jitters.
Social injustice reveals the bigotry that mars the unity of our country.
What do we do about this anger?
We must use it constructively.
That is, for common cause.
Use it as energy to build something better, a more equitable society.
One that is more just.
Anger raised in hatred is destructive.
Anger raised for love is righteous.

WORK TO STAY CONNECTED

One of my favorite poets is Ted Kooser.
He's from Nebraska,and he was a poet laureate for our country
as well as a Pulitzer Prize winner for poetry.
He wrote a poem called "The Mourners"
about people gathering at a funeral.
They meet and greet and shake hands.
It is kind of where we're at right now.
Except in our world, we don't have the gift of touch.

We are isolated.
We are separated from one another.
But amid our losses,
whether it be a loss of a loved one, or a loss of work,
or the loss of a colleague, we can rejuvenate ourselves
by staying connected to those who matter the most to us.
You must make the effort to connect,
to become more visible.

A leader's job, says my colleague Ron Carucci,
is to enable others to "feel your presence." [1]
Communicate via words and deeds.
Let people know that you have their back.
It is a matter of connection.

FIGHTING DISCOURAGEMENT

Discouragement.
That's a popular word at times.
People are pretty annoyed about their situation.
Not at any one individual, of course, but at the situation itself.
We want to get on with our lives.
The sad truth is that the lives we knew at the beginning of this year
are not coming back as we had expected. Or will expect.
Leaders must address that discouragement.

As my London colleague Alex Lazarus says, [2]
you have to meet people where they are.
Understand their needs.
And that's a challenge to leaders.
You need to listen, double down on listening,
listening for the personal side.
Discouragement.
It's the enemy of any progress.
It's the enemy of our future.
Address it.

MIND YOUR CULTURE

How is your culture?
I know that's a question that a lot of executives are asking themselves,
as they consider the impact that the crisis is provoking on their culture.

Culture is our set of norms and values that we hold dear.
It governs our behaviors, how we interact with one another.
And now that some of us are in an office,
and some are working remotely,
what is that going to mean for the future of our culture?

Proximity to power has always been a ticket to getting noticed.
But how do you become noticed if you're working virtually?

That's something that executives need to pay attention to.
How do they keep their eye out for talent
when that talent is working virtually?

Just how *is* our culture?
We must keep asking.

FINDING NEW OPPORTUNITIES

Now, who would buy used golf balls?
Well, I would.
But I got to thinking, each one of these balls represents a mistake.
People don't trade in golf balls.
They lose them.
Each one of these balls was either found in the rough, or the woods,
or behind a tree… or at the bottom of a pond.

People like me can buy these balls cheaply
and use them in our own games.
And I do.
I've actually done okay with these used balls.
My game is not stellar.
I've turned some of these balls into my own pars.
I've also turned them into a birdie.
And yes, I've lost them.

The reason I'm talking about lost golf balls, or used golf balls,
is because I think it's a good metaphor for our times.
We're in an upside-down world.
What at first seems like a problem
might just turn out to be an opportunity.
Think about your own life and your business career.
Are there some used golf balls you might buy?
How can you turn them into an opportunity that benefits yourself,
your team, and your organization?

WE'RE ALL IN THIS TOGETHER

Every crisis, perhaps, carries a silver lining.
I think that people are more kind to one another.
While tension surrounds, it does not suffocate us.
I see that people are cutting one another a little bit of slack.
It is the sense that we're all in this together.
You can go around being angry, irritated, furious even.
And there are righteous reasons to feel so.
People are acting with kindness.
They're looking at other folks with more of an open heart…
because we're all experiencing this crisis in different ways.
I think we're more willing to give one another break.
If there's anything good in this crisis—and there's very little—
I think there is this sense of, again, shared sacrifice…
and the willingness to be more kind to one another.

GRATITUDE FOR SELF

What are you grateful for?
A couple of friends of mine, Adrian Gostick and Chester Elton,
wrote an excellent book called *Leading with Gratitude.*[3]
And that is a compelling concept of showing appreciation for others
and doing it with real meaning.
There's another form of gratefulness.
And that's being grateful for oneself… for the talents you have,
for the skills you have.
That's not an exercise in braggadocio. It is an exercise of fulfillment.

It is knowing that *I have these talents. I have these skills.*
What can I do with them?
Certainly, you put them to use in your own career to advance.
But, how can you help others with the talents and skills that you have?
That's another form of expressing gratitude.
Gratitude is essential for our lives…
Especially now, when so often

we're physically distant from one another.

It is important to express gratitude and to put it into action.

PATIENCE

They say that patience is a virtue.

If that's so, it's a virtue that I don't possess.

Patience is something I struggle with on a daily basis.

And now, in our time of crisis,

when nerves get a little frayed and tensions rise,

patience can be hard to practice.

Practice it; we must.

Patience is that ability—our mastery of ourselves over events.

We don't control events, but we control how we react to them.

We can get better with patience

through deep breathing, yoga exercises, or just regular exercises.

Patience begins with a commitment to master your emotions.

RESILIENCE

I've always thought of resilience as that ability to snap back from defeat.

And it is. It is "bouncing back."

At the same time, Eileen McDargh has an interesting theory about it.

She calls it bouncing forward.

And my friend Jesse Lynn Stoner talks about it as "re-shaping ourselves." [4]

The world that we've left behind in the early part of this year

isn't going to come back.

We will come back in a new form.

We will bounce forward.

It is good to think about resilience as that opportunity.

Also, if you're going to bounce forward to reinvent yourself,

focus your energy on doing something different.

How you can make yourself better in what it is you do.

MANAGING DOUBT

Our world has been turned upside down.
We live in a world of uncertainty…
a world of ambiguity that makes a lot of us uncomfortable.
It gives rise to doubt.
And traditionally, certainly in the business community, doubt is
sometimes shunned as a weakness
when actually it's a strength.
Doubt is a way of protecting ourselves.
Doubt is a way of challenging our assumptions, our beliefs, our norms.
Doubt can be our best friend in times of uncertainty
because it causes us to be a little more cautious, a little more careful.

For leaders that degree of caution, that degree of care, is good.
Of course, if you're paralyzed by doubt, it's not good.
But when considered wisely, doubt can be a good companion.

ENERGY

Energy is the life force of any team of any organization.
How does a leader deliver energy,
especially when she or he is working apart from the team?
There are many ways to do it.
First, you have to keep yourself recharged and rejuvenated.
And you know ways to do that.

But the other way is to ask people what they want from you.

How can you show them that you are there for them?
How can you be that spark plug of energy?
By asking them, you invite them to contribute.
And in doing so, you build a more cohesive team.

PUT OTHERS FIRST

What does it mean to lead and to put others first?
I came up with a little mantra that I have used for years,
and shared with all of my coaching clients.
It has three things: Be seen. Be heard. Be there.

Be seen is to be visible.
And even when you're in an isolated location, you can be seen on screen.

Be heard.
Make sure the message that the team needs to hear is consistent.
And part of that hearing is listening.
Listening to what people say and listening to what you don't hear.

And the third part is probably the most important... be there!
Be there is the all-encompassing thought.
It means to be accessible, be available.
Be whatever the team needs you to do to help everyone succeed.

Be seen. Be heard. Be there.
That's what it means to put others first when you lead.

ASK YOUR PEOPLE TO THINK ALONG WITH YOU

I had a remarkable conversation with a CEO who I've known
for quite some time, Jim Haudan of Root, Inc.[5]
We were talking about leading in a crisis.
And one of the things Jim said is that it is essential to acknowledge the
anxiety people feel.
But he also talked about a theme that I've talked about before, and
that's working with your people.

Jim used the word "co-think."
It's an inviting concept--bringing people together to think together.
Thinking together leads to creation,
and to collaboration.
Co-thinking is the platform.
That's the basics. That's where it begins.
It is an inviting concept.
And when you do it as a leader,
it means you regard your employee as one from whom you can learn.
Someone who can help our organization move forward.

RESPECT

Respect is the ability to look at another person as someone who is a
whole person.
Respect is a way of getting rid of any prejudice we have for them.
It requires looking at individuals and giving them
the benefit of the doubt.
Looking at what they can do rather than what you think they might do.
Now, of course, in a team environment...
we know one another's strengths and weaknesses.
But it is necessary for leaders to demonstrate respect for others.
You show that respect by listening to them
and giving them appropriate levels of responsibility.
That's it for now.

COMPASSION

Compassion is rooted in a sense of passion for other people.
Compassion is concern and caring.
Leaders need to make it known
that they care about individuals on their team as people…
as contributors, and as potential collaborators.
Compassion is the way of looking at the individual as a whole person.
As someone who can contribute
and make others better through his or her actions.
Compassion is what we need in times of crisis…
because it is the demonstrated concern for others.

III.

RE-MINDFULNESS

I was on a a conference call with my friend Marshall Goldsmith,[6]
talking about mindfulness.
Marshall laughed and said that
while he practiced mindfulness,
one of the things he struggled with was remembering something.
I came up with the word "re-mindfulness."

Kind of a silly term,
but it made me think a little more deeply
of how we might remind ourselves,
especially in a time of crisis,
of the right things we have around us… our family, our friends.
And this reminds us that we're here to help others
and of the ways we all have to help someone…
to reach out and "touch" them, speaking metaphorically.
Talk to them. Reach out via text, telephone, video chat.
Be connected to other people.
It's a good "re-mindfulness" lesson.

KINDNESS

We've all heard the term "random acts of kindness."
I prefer something a little more direct...
I call it *intended* acts of kindness.
That is developing a mindset where you can be of assistance, of help,
be a source of joy to someone else.
By thinking this way, you adopt a kindness mindset.
You get out of your own skin, and you walk in the shoes of another,
if only for a moment.
It's other-directedness that I think we all need.

To be thinking of one another
and also finding ways to deliver joy.
And to deliver an act of kindness,
something that puts a smile on someone else's face.
It doesn't have to be a big thing.
An emoji text.
A funny photograph.
It could be a joke that you've heard... or a happy story. Simple things.
These are acts of kindness.
Little things show others that you're thinking of them, and
that you care about them as fellow travelers.

EMPATHY

We need to know others care about us.
We call it empathy.
Empathy is the ability to share
and understand another's feelings.
A leader needs to demonstrate concern
and understand what people are going through,
especially if your workers are working from home with children.
They have a lot of concerns aside from work.

Leaders show empathy, particularly in times of loss.
To show concern for suffering, and that's where empathy comes in.
There's another aspect of empathy, and that's sharing in the joy.
There are good things happening.
Empathy cuts both ways.
It is up to leaders to demonstrate it.

JOY

One of the things we forget to notice when we're in a crisis
is the simple feeling of joy.
Joy can be an enriching experience, especially when you're feeling tense.
For leaders, it is crucial to find ways to celebrate the good things.
Celebrate activities that people are doing, taking note of them,
recognizing them,
but also doing so in a spirit that gives people happiness.
That's a way to deliver joy.

When we're feeling down,
when we're feeling depressed…
joy can be that leavening experience.
It raises us up.
And makes us feel better about who we are as a people,
as a team.
Joy enriches our souls.

CALL ME OUT

My wife told me about a conversation she had with a young colleague
in her office.
My wife asked her if she felt comfortable enough to raise serious issues,
be it about race, gender equity, or other issues that affect the workplace.
And the young woman was not certain,
"Well," my wife replied, "it's my responsibility to enable you to
'call me out.'"
That's a good lesson for all of us, especially those in leadership,
to make it safe to have those tough conversations,
but also to "call people out" when it is a matter of values.
Because when you do that,
you create an atmosphere where people feel that they belong,
and that their voice can be heard.
I think that's important.
"Call me out."
It's a good lesson for every leader.

STAY CONNECTED

What else is there to say about what it takes to lead in the pandemic?
You've said everything you can say.
You've given your inspirational speech.
You've stayed in touch with your people.
But what else?

The most important, of course, is your example, and you know that.
But a part of that example is staying connected.
I think now, in times of crisis, people need one another more than ever.
We need to feel a kinship with others.
Are you connecting with them?
Are you there for them?
When times are tough people want to know
that leaders have their backs.
They want to know that leaders will stand up for them.

That's part of what it means to be connected.
Stand tall for your people.
Be available to them. Be accessible.
Listen to them.
We need to stay connected.
And leaders can do that by being available, by being accessible,
by listening.
Stay connected with your folks.

LABOR DAY

I've always thought of Labor Day as a second New Year's Day.
That likely goes back to my days as a school kid when we started school
after Labor Day.
Now, in the business world, in the adult world,
we're thinking about planning for the end of the year, but also thinking
about the next year.
What do you need to do to close out the year on a positive note?

Encourage your people to stay healthy, to get a flu vaccine.
From a business angle, what can you do to fulfill your final objectives?
In a team sense, what do you do to bring people closer together?
How can they collaborate virtually?
How do we work more effectively as a team?
Big questions. Big priorities.
Labor Day is that time to plan for the end of the year, and for the next.

LINCOLN STORIES

One of my heroes is Abraham Lincoln.
And while we know he was an exceptional leader,
he was also a great raconteur.
It is a skill he polished as a circuit rider lawyer,
going from town to town in the Illinois backwoods.
He took that gift with him to the White House.
And during the darkest days of the Civil War,
he entertained himself and others with great storytelling.
Lincoln's example is something we can keep in mind today
when we're isolating.
Share stories that make you cry,
stories that make you think,
and stories that make you laugh.
We all need a good story.

HOPE

When times are tough, people want hope.
And why not?
Because it might be the only thing, they have.
How do leaders respond to this need for hope?
Especially when times are so challenging and you don't have an answer.
I think the best thing is that, yes, you deliver hope.
But you do it with a sense of realism.

You turn the equation back on itself.
I have hope in us.
I have faith in us.
I believe that together we can survive.
I believe that we will make things work.
That's a way of framing hope in a realistic way.
We all want hope.
The challenge is making it come true.

NEXT FOR ME (SECOND THOUGHTS)

Living as we are going through the greatest crisis of recent memory,
it is natural to be thinking:
Should I be doing something different?
Do I want to continue in my career?
For some of us, the answer is easy.
We love what we do.

There are others, even successful people in their careers,
that will think, *I'd like to do something different.*
Now is the time to think about those options.

Whether you're late-career, mid-career, or early career,
it's always wise to consider what you can do differently.
If only to make what you're doing now more challenging…
and to explore how you can be of greater service to others.
Make time now to think about what you could be doing differently.
It's a good question to ask,
and it'll help you think through the next steps
of your life and your career.

STEP TO THE FORE

When trouble strikes, it is an opportunity for leaders to step to the fore.
This is how and where they show their mettle,
what they can do for others.
Crisis provokes opportunity.
It provokes the opportunity, at a minimum, to change.
Leaders call upon others to come together for a common cause…
be that cause of your business, your organization, your community.
Whatever it is, the time to act is now.
People are looking for direction.
People are looking for leadership.
People are looking for hope.
And leaders have the opportunity to deliver that.
As you look forward, and times seem to get tight and tighter,
and tensions rise…
Now's the opportunity for leaders to step to the fore.

PATIENCE FOR OPPORTUNITY

"It's not just about speed. It's about patience."
Those words come from a film, *Ride Like a Girl*.
And while they pertain to horse racing,
those words are right for our times.
Some of us like to jump in and make things happen, which is good.
But sometimes we need to just hang back a bit.
Wait for opportunities to arise.
And that's where patience comes in.
Patience isn't always easy. I know it isn't for me.
But patience may be what your team needs you to do.
To consider the options, to retest your assumptions.
Patience is something that we all need to develop,
especially in times of crisis, when the impetus to act is powerful.
But sometimes, hanging back just a bit,
allows for better opportunities to emerge.

QUESTIONS FOR THE "NEW NORMAL" WORKPLACE

I have two questions.
What will the future of work be like?
And what will the future hold for those who work virtually?
These are big questions, because we are going back to work already.
It looks like more and more people will opt to work from home.
But will that give them a disadvantage
when it comes to opportunities for promotion?
Because likely the bosses will be in an office
when a worker is not in the office.
There is a kind of a "not seen and not heard" mentality.
You may be overlooked for promotions,
or added forms of responsibility.

What steps will management take
to ensure that workers who work from home
are still considered part of the team?
Ph.D. candidates will write dissertations on these questions.
But leaders need to ask these questions now.
They must create a workforce where everyone has a role to play.
Because right now, we need all hands on deck.

ABUNDANCE

There's a word that makes me smile every time I hear it.
The word is abundance.
It is imperative in our time of crisis,
when our natural default is to protect.
And that means scarcity.
Many people are stepping forward and sharing.
And that's where the spirit of abundance comes from.

Abundance is rooted in Grace.
Because it means working for the greater good.
And when you have a spirit of abundance, you want to share.

All of us have something we can share.
It may be a resource. It may be our time…
it may be our experience, or maybe a story.
Abundance is an attitude that says
We're all in this together and *let's pull together.*

LAUGHTER

My wife and I sat down
and watched Jerry Seinfeld's Netflix special, *23 Hours to Kill.*
We both roared with laughter.
And what a joy!
We were both laughing about it the next day.
It was a reminder that even in tough times,
it's so important to laugh.

Two heroes of mine, Abraham Lincoln and Franklin Roosevelt,
laughed when times were terrible.
Leaders must indulge in laughter, and
to share that laughter with others.
Laughter is an affirmation of who we are as a people.
Spread it widely. Share it generously.

MAKING PERSONAL CHANGE

Change begins one person at a time.
And it begins with ourselves.
Assume the best intentions of others.
Look for ways to turn negative thoughts into positive actions.
Turn these kinds of things into making a positive difference for others.
Maybe you want to volunteer in your community.
And the other thing is to think and act more positively in general.

My philosophy is anchored in the notion of Grace,
which I regard as the catalyst for positive change.
Use Grace to reach out to others to make genuine connections.
We suffer together. We persist together.
We will emerge, let's hope, a better people.
But if we are, it will involve personal change.
Each of us is doing what we can.

MARK THE MOMENT

Tasha Eurich told me recently how proud she was
of what executives she knew were doing. [7]
These leaders kept their organizations together
under trying circumstances.
They've made tough decisions.
They've rallied people, brought them together for a common cause.
We're all dealing with circumstances we didn't anticipate or welcome.

We're making the best of it.
Now might be a time to celebrate, if you will,
what you've accomplished.
It may not always be what you wanted.
But it's time to take a note of reflection,
and say "Hey, we did the best we could."
It's up to the leader. It's up to the team.
Working together.

INSPIRATION

People look to their leaders for something special, something extra.
We call it inspiration.
The word inspiration comes from the Latin "spiritus,"
which is "vigor, soul, courage, breath."
It also has a derivation from Ecclesiastical Latin,
which is "spirare," which is "to breathe, to breathe out."
And if we think about inspiration
as both courage and a breaking in… and breathing out.
it helps us get a handle on what leaders can do.

They share what they have with others.
They give us courage.
And they do it through their example.
They do it through their words.
They lift us up.
They give us something bigger than ourselves to believe in.
Inspiration. It is a fundamental concept.
And we need it now more than ever.

VALUES

Change is all around us.
The pandemic and it accompanying crises
have altered everything around us.
And as we consider what comes next,
let's remember that the world we're shaping now
will be based on the values we hold dear now.
Let's assert our values—the things that are important to us.
Let's hang onto them.
Let's put them to good use.
Our values have held us in good stead previously.
And they'll hold us in good stead as we go forward.

IV.

BUILD IT BETTER

Something that you hear businesspeople and government officials
talk about in the wake of our crisis is to rebuild.
But not just rebuild but to "build it better."
What does that mean for us in the role of human development?
I think that we can take this concept of "better" and apply it to
processes but also to organizational culture.

How can we make our cultures more inclusive?
How can we reward people more generously,
as well as more equitably?
How do we provide greater opportunities for people in the office space,
and in virtual spaces?
What can we do to make our business better?
These are all important questions
that must be asked as we find ways to "build it better."[9]

LEAD WITH COURAGE

We see examples of courage all around us.
People putting themselves at risk to help others.
You show courage by standing up for your people,
by advocating for their needs, by supporting them…
by going the extra mile for them.
You become their champion.
You extol their deeds.
You honor their sacrifice.
You commend their fortitude.
Courage is critical.
Now and for our future.

TRUST YOUR TEAM

My colleague Jesse Lynn Stoner told me how important it is for teams
to pull together during tough times.[9]
While we speak about a leader's responsibility for bringing the
organization together, individuals and teams have a role, too.
Jesse said when you work with a very effective team,
you may not know who the team leader is because everyone's working
cooperatively and collaboratively.
Good teams find ways to remain connected, add new members, and
find new ways of doing things.
The strength of our teams will enable us to navigate tough times.

GENEROSITY

Generosity is that open-hearted spirit.
It is the willingness to embrace others… to meet them where they are.
And to demonstrate that you care about them
and are willing to be open-hearted.
And to work for the benefit of all.
Generous people give of themselves.

They give their time.
And they also encourage others to do the same.
Not because they have to, but because they want to.
I like to say that generosity is contagious.
When we see one person acting generously,
we are moved to do the same.

HUMOR AND CONNECTIONS

Is This Anything? is a collection of Jerry Seinfeld's
stand-up bits stretching back to the 1970s.
Seinfeld is a master of observational comedy.
Which is looking at everyday life and finding the fun
or the humor in it.
I think we can all use a little dose of humor these days.
And there's something else in the book that Jerry talks about.
It is the personal connection he feels with his audiences.
And that's something else we need in our lives.

We need connections.
Jerry does it through his comedy.
The question is:
How are we making connections?
How are we connecting to others?
How are we connecting to our work?
How are we connecting to what matters most in our lives?
A little bit of humor goes a long way and also makes a connection.

REBUILD WITH CONFIDENCE

How should leaders approach the new year?

Acknowledge all the excellent efforts that your people have made.

Against terrible odds, all of you have survived.

You're probably not in a better position, but you survived.

I think you've learned some things about yourself.

You learned about resilience.

And how when people pull together, they can accomplish good things, even great things.

Talk to your people.

Ask them what their expectations are for the coming year.

See what you can do to help them make these things come true.

Make the coming year a rebuilding year, a year where we pulled together and made good things happen.

FOCUS ON BETTER

It's no secret that new year's resolutions often fail.

At least they do for me.

But the idea of improving oneself is sound, we should all strive for that.

Here's my idea: "Focus on better."

Now, here's the good part about it.

You define what "better" means for you.

Be better at work. Be a better colleague.

Be a better spouse. Be a better friend.

Pick whatever it is you want to do.

Then ask: how could I do it more effectively?

How could I be more helpful to a colleague?

In other words, you define what better means to you and act upon it.

Do so with the knowledge that what you choose is an aspiration.

You may fall short, but at least promise it to yourself.

And that's where the better part comes in.

You'll do "better" than next time.

LOVE FOR EACH OTHER

There is a famous quote from the legendary football coach,
Vince Lombardi.
"I don't necessarily have to like my players and associates," he said.
"But as their leader, I must love them.
Love is loyalty.
Love is teamwork.
Love respects the dignity of the individual.
This is the strength of any organization."

Lombardi hits the nail on the head.
Love is a matter of respect.
And when you show respect to people, you demonstrate that you care about them
And in return, they will show you loyalty.
Not because they have to, but because they want to.
Because you know what?
They will love you in return.

THE POWER TO HEAL

Wither Grace?
We live in contentious times.
Grace has never been more necessary.
The elements of Grace are that it facilitates connectedness.
It facilitates doing good.
Grace, by its nature, is given without strings attached.
At the same time, Grace involves mercy and forgiveness.
We show mercy toward those who are against us…
and we also forgive those who wronged us.
Grace does not preclude accountability.
It demands it.

Because Grace is that power for good.
And if we are going to heal,
there must be a degree of acknowledgment of our wrongdoings,
and resolving to do better.
Grace is necessary if we're going to move forward.
It is necessary for forgiveness.
It is necessary for mercy.
But again, it can reinforce accountability.

Why?
Because Grace has that extraordinary power that enables us
to acknowledge our shortcomings.
We can forgive ourselves.
Grace is kind of a mysterious connectedness
that we can all share with one another.
And, at the same time, it can be a force that facilitates good.

EPILOGUE

The little boy, just two, stood and stared.
In disbelief.
His look was not of sadness.
It was dismay.
How could you?
You just got here!
Even after he had pulled on his Gee–Ma's coat.
Off, off, he said. (Meaning stay, stay.)
But she could not.
A fleeting visit, too hurried.
And off she went back into the gloom we call Covid.

WHAT WE ENDURED

It did not happen suddenly.
Reports from Wuhan about a novel coronavirus made some news.
When the virus struck Italy, people asked:
"Was this a real-life case of *Contagion*,
the movie about a pandemic emanating from China?"
In short order, the virus spread to Washington, Oregon,
California and New York.
Then it was everywhere.

From March on, the days became a blur.
Blursday as the Oxford English dictionary noted it.
Minutes clicked. Seconds dragged.
Hours dragged into days.
Even digital clocks seemed still.
Wearing and weary, we persisted.
Blursday after Blursday.

Boundaries no more between home and work.
Some made the shift to virtual without missing a step.
Others stumbled, tripped and fell flat.
Yet time at work, at home, sped up.
Zoom at dawn.
Zoom at noon.
Zoom at dusk.
Zoom, Zoom, Zoom.
I read somewhere that the CEO of Zoom never intended for Zoom to
be like this.
Easy for him to say.
Zoom is here to stay.

At work we toiled on screen.
Pivot became our watchword.
Become virtual, we said.
Talked to a screen.
Stared at a screen.

Screamed at a screen.
Always on. Always there.
Was this our new companion, a kind of avatar?
One without warmth. Just a cold stare.
There, there, there.

Kids rootless now.
No school. They, too, on Zoom.
For some it was a breeze. For others a struggle.
For moms and dads, a relentless push.
Pull. And push.
To keep them focused. On track. And learning.
Learning? We hoped.

Isolation and disconnection became our norm.
No longer meeting for coffee over break.
Or seeing friends for drinks.
Those residing in a single domicile were the fortunate ones.
Hugs and kisses were still allowed.
Those alone had no such luck.
Just their solitude to keep them company.

I attended a wedding. Via Zoom.
The many gathered virtually, listened intently
As vows were exchanged.
Those present clapped and cheered.
And those far away smiled and some even shed a tear.
United in spirit. Virtually.

Social hour became virtual, too.
Virtual cocktails. Virtual dinners.
Virtual, virtual, virtual.
As the joke goes, the only thing worse than being virtual
is not being virtual at all.
Count your blessings.
You still had your friends.

WHAT WE SAW

Our televisions brought our sordid history back to life.
The asphyxiation of George Floyd by a white police officer
reminded us again how little some lives do matter.
It was one of many such killings. White cop on unarmed Black civilian.
This time it was different.
We saw it on television. Again. Again and again.
Seemingly non-stop.
People took to the streets to protest.
There was order mostly and some were joined by the police themselves.
Yet there was disorder, too. Looting and destruction.

Something else, though, a footnote perhaps.
So many doing the reporting, the arresting, the adjudicating and the
pontificating were themselves Black.
Surely, we were better than our forefathers?
Maybe!

We were awakened, as we have been before to the injustice that lies
before us.
Social justice cannot be cured with more laws, more protections.
It must come from our sense of "peoplehood."
If Covid has taught us one thing, it is that we are all in this together.
White. Black. Brown. Yellow. Red. And every shade in between.

Calling themselves patriots, insurrectionists besieged the U.S. Capitol.
Their presence was an ugly reminder of the divisions that separate us.
Nothing good can occur when people who traffic in violence are
allowed to riot.

Covid, too, has given us the opportunity to think, rethink really,
who we want to become.
Society must change, we agree.
But no change can occur without a look in the mirror.
The change we seek must come from a reflection
on how we think, feel, and act.

Bias is our protection, we think.
It shields us from having to think more deeply about the injustice around us.
It's not my problem, our bias tells us. It is "their problem."
Wrong, of course, the mirror does not lie.

WHAT WE LOST

Ourselves mostly.
What we imagined for ourselves once, no longer seemed so sure.
Once we counted on this and that.
Now we know "this and that" are no more.

We lost our security.
Our illusion of destiny.
A life planned is an illusion, after all.
"Man plans, God laughs" goes the saying.
Never more true than now.

Colleagues have moved on.
Their jobs no more.
We feel sad for them, but secretly breathe relief.
"I am still here."

We lost civility, too.
Those who did not wear masks taunted those who did.
And vice versa.
Meanwhile Covid cases continue to rise by the millions.

We lost friends.
Covid does not play favorites.
The losses mount.
Day after day.
First, we lost as many as were lost on 9/11.
Then all those who were killed in Vietnam.
Next Korea. And World War I and II.
What does it matter to compare?
We lost people.
"An empty chair," our new president reminds us.

I attended a funeral. By Zoom.
The handful of mourners present at graveside
Were dwarfed by the hundreds watching via Zoom.
Less a funeral and more a celebration of life.
Moving all the same.
The loss is there. Felt by all. Even on the Zoom.

WHAT WE GAINED
Resilience.
We learned we can get knocked down. Hard.
And get back up again.
More vulnerable, more humble now, yes.
And more courageous,more alive, too.

Resilience is our tool for reinvention.
We become transformed.
The world we left behind is no more.
It is up to us to create what we like to call the "new normal."

We gained also, a sense of ourselves.
Who we are as a people.
Friends. Colleagues. Families.
Husbands. Wives.
All brothers and sisters in creating something different.
We do seem altered as a people.

Living with a plague can do that to you.
Yes, we saw vitriol, but we also witnessed more Grace. Much more.
We saw neighbor helping neighbor, and strangers helping strangers.
Communities reaching out to those in need.
And lastly there is hope.
Holding us tight as we hold on to it.
We feel it.
We embrace it.
We even hope for it.
Hope is like that.

We hope for something better.
To go outside and breathe deeply without fear.
To mingle with others without fear.
To congregate for worship, or for play.

We need hope. It sustains us all.

The boy of two smiles now.
His Gee-Ma has returned.
All vaxxed up, coat off and ready to play.
Smiles.
Laughter.
Joy.
We have survived.

END NOTES

1 Ron Carucci, CEO of Navalent, a leadership development firm, is a best-selling author.

2 Alex Lazarus is an executive coach and leadership consultant based in London.

3 Adrian Gostick and Chester Elton are founders of The Culture Works and have written a number of New York Times and Wall Street Journal best-selling books.

4 Eileen McDargh and Jesse Lyn Stoner are authors and organizational development consultants.

5 Jim Haudan is the CEO of Root, Inc, a vision and strategy firm, located in Maumee, Ohio.

6 Marshall Goldsmith, Ph.D., is the preeminent executive coach in the world and the author of many books.

7 Tasha Eurich, Ph.D., is a researcher and best-selling author of *Insight*.

8 Inspiration for "build it better" comes from Mark C. Thompson, an entrepreneur, author and executive coach.

ACKNOWLEDGEMENTS

This book was born in a time of plague. When I am faced with an existential crisis, I am spurred to create. This book grew out of the series of short videos I did as part of my effort to help leaders to deal with the crisis. In reality what I was doing was helping myself process the madness that had turned our world upside down.

This book owes a debt of gratitude to Marshall Goldsmith 100 Coaches, a group of thought leaders and doers who work to help leaders become better leaders. It is founded on the principles of pay-it-forward by which Marshall abides. As Marshall likes to say, "'Learn as much as you can. Help as much as you can."

Members who have helped me develop the ideas in this book include John Strelecky, C.B. Bowman, Scott Osman, Chester Elton, Adrian Gostick, Morag Barrett, Cynthia Burnham, Howard Prager, Evelyn Rodstein, Rhett Power, Shannon Polson, Sally Helgesen, Oleg Konovalov, Louis Carter, David Nour, Alaina Love, Lacey Leone McLaughlin, Deepa Prahalad, Ron Carucci, Alex Lazarus, Harry Kraemer, Jr. Tasha Eurich, Dorie Clark and Alisa Cohn. Likely I have forgotten to mention someone and I am sorry. The omission is due to my faulty memory not my intention.

And, as with every book, I owe a debt of gratitude to my wife, Gail Campanella. Her leadership of her team during this crisis inspired me. Every day she reached out to her team, individually and collectively, to provide them the guidance and the support good leaders deliver. I also appreciate her patience in putting up with me through the long months of this crisis.

ABOUT JOHN BALDONI

John Baldoni is a globally recognized leadership educator, certified Master Corporate Executive Coach, and author of fifteen books that have been translated into ten languages.

John's books include G*RACE: A Leader's Guide to a Better Us,* *MOXIE: The Secret to Bold and Gutsy Leadership, Lead with Purpose,* *Lead Your Boss,* and *The Leader's Pocket Guide.*

In 2021, the International Federation of Learning and Development named John a World-Class Mentor and named him to its Hall of Fame. In 2020 Global Gurus ranked John a Top 30 global leadership expert, a list he has been on since 2007. In 2018, Inc.com named John a Top 100 speaker, and Trust Across America honored John with its Lifetime Achievement Award for Trust. In 2014 Inc.com listed John as a Top 50 leadership expert.

John is also a member of the renowned Marshall Goldsmith 100 coaches, a group of executive coaches and thought leaders from the worlds of business, academia and social service.

John established a career as a highly sought-after executive coach, where he has had the privilege of working with senior leaders in virtually every industry from pharmaceutical to real estate, packaged goods to automobiles, and finance to healthcare.

John has authored more than 800 leadership columns for a variety of online publications including *Forbes, Harvard Business Review* and *Inc.com* John also produced and appears in a video coaching series for SmartBrief, a news channel with an audience of more than 6 million. John is also the host of LinkedIn Live's *Grace Under Pressure* interview series. John's leadership resource website is www.johnbaldoni.com